WE WORSHIP AND ADORE YOU

Songbook

"Speak to one another with psalms, hymns and spiritual songs.
Sing and make music in your heart to the Lord,
Always giving thanks to God the Father for everything,
In the name of our Lord Jesus Christ"

Ephesians 5:19-20

Published 2000
All rights reserved.

No part of this songbook or any other Holy Trinity Brompton
resource may be reproduced or transmitted in any form or by any
means, electronic or mechanical, including photocopying, recording, or
any information and retrieval system, without permission in writing
from the copyright holder or the expressly authorised agent thereof.

Published by HTB Publications
Holy Trinity Brompton, Brompton Road, London SW7 1JA

Contents

		full score	guitar sheets	acetate masters
•	Here we stand..	4	37/38	59
•	Lord, You are calling.....................................	7	39	60
•	Breathe on me, breath of God	10	40	61
•	By His grace	11	41	62
•	Faithful One	12	42	63
•	I will worship	14	43	64
•	Overwhelmed by love	16	44	65
•	Father God, fill this place	18	45/46	66
•	Let all the world	20	47	67
•	We worship and adore You	21	48/49	68
•	The Lord is my light.....................................	23	50/51	69
•	My Jesus, my Saviour	26	52/53	70
•	Our Father	28	54	71
•	I will offer up my life....................................	30	55	72
•	Jesus Christ	32	56	73
•	In my life, Lord	34	57	74
•	Rain and snow fall from the sky	35	58	75

HERE WE STAND

A. Piercy & C. Groves

Verse
1. Here we stand in total surrender, lifting our voices, abandoned to Your cause; here we stand, praying in the glory of the One and only Jesus Christ the Lord.

Chorus
This time revival; Lord, come and heal

Copyright © 1995 IQ Music Limited,
Orchard House, Broad Street, Tylers Green, Cuckfield, West Sussex, RH17 5DZ, UK. Used by permission.

our land, bring to completion the work that You've begun. This time revival stir up Your church again, pour out Your Spirit on Your daughters and Your sons.

Last time
To continue

Verse
2. Here we stand in need of Your mercy,

Fa - ther for - give us for the time that we have lost.

Once a - gain make us an ar - my to con-quer this

na - tion with the mes - sage of the cross. This time re-

LORD YOU ARE CALLING

Simon & Lorraine Fenner

1. Lord, You are calling the people of Your Kingdom to battle in Your name against the enemy. To stand before You, a people who will serve You, 'til Your Kingdom is released throughout the earth. Let Your

Copyright © 1989 Kingsway's Thankyou Music,
P.O. Box 75, Eastbourne, East Sussex, BN23 6NW, UK. Used by permission.

G C D Em C
17 King - dom come let Your will be done on
Am Am/G 1. Dsus4 D 2. Dsus4
21 earth as it is in hea - ven. Let Your hea -
D Last time Em To continue Em D/E
26 ven.
Em Verse D
32 2. At the name of Je - sus ev - 'ry knee must bow; the

darkness of this age must flee a-way.

Release Your power to flow through-out the land, let Your

glory be revealed as we praise. Let Your

9

BREATHE ON ME, BREATH OF GOD

Words: Edwin Hatch
Music: Charles Lockhart

1. Breathe on me, breath of God, fill me with life anew, that I may love what Thou dost love and do what Thou wouldst do.
2. Breathe on me, breath of God, until my heart is pure: until my will is one with Thine, to do and to endure.
3. Breathe on me, breath of God, till I am wholly Thine, until this earthly part of me glows with Thy fire divine.
4. Breathe on me, breath of God, so shall I never die, but live with Thee the perfect life of Thine eternity.

Public Domain

BY HIS GRACE

Steven Fry

By His grace I am re-deemed, by His blood I am made clean, and I now can know Him face to face. By His pow'r I have been raised, hid-den now in Christ by faith. I will praise the glo-ry of His grace.

Copyright © 1994 Deep Fryed Music/Music Services. Administered by CopyCare,
P.O. Box 77, Hailsham, East Sussex, BN27 3EF, UK. Used by permission.

FAITHFUL ONE

Brian Doerksen

Faith-ful One, so un-chang-ing, age-less One, You're my rock of peace. Lord of all, I de-pend on You, I call out to You a-gain and a-gain, I call out to You a-gain and a-

Copyright © 1987 Mercy Publishing/Kingsway's Thankyou Music,
P.O. Box 75, Eastbourne, East Sussex, BN23 6NW, UK. Used by permission.

13

I WILL WORSHIP

David Ruis

Verse

1. I will worship (I will worship) with all of my heart. (with all of my heart.)
I will praise You (I will praise You) with all of my strength. (all my strength)
I will seek You (I will seek You) all of my days. (all of my days.)
I will fol-low (I will fol-low) all of Your ways. (all Your ways.)

Copyright © 1993 Shade Tree Music/Maranatha! Music. Administered by CopyCare,
P.O. Box 77, Hailsham, East Sussex, BN27 3EF, UK. Used by permission.

2. I will bow down, (echo)
   Hail You as king. (echo)
   I will serve You, (echo)
   Give You everything.
   (Give You everything.)
   I will lift up (echo)
   My eyes to Your throne. (echo)
   I will trust You, (echo)
   I will trust You alone.
   (You alone.)

OVERWHELMED BY LOVE

Noel Richards

1. O-ver-whelmed by love, deep-er than o-ceans, high as the heav-ens. Ev-er liv-ing God, Your love has res-cued me.

2. All my sin was laid on Your dear Son, Your pre-cious one. All my debt He paid, great is Your love for me.

Chorus
No one could ev-er earn Your love, Your grace and

Copyright © 1994 Kingsway's Thankyou Music,
P.O. Box 75, Eastbourne, East Sussex, BN23 6NW, UK. Used by permission.

mer - cy is free. Lord, these words are true, so is my love for You, so is my love for You.

FATHER GOD, FILL THIS PLACE

Dave Bilbrough

1. Fa - ther God, fill this place with Your love, with Your grace. As we call on Your name, vi - sit us in pow'r a - gain.

2. Spi - rit come heal our wounds, bring re - lease. Lord, we long for Your touch, fill our hearts with Your love.

Copyright © 1995 Kingsway's Thankyou Music,
P.O. Box 75, Eastbourne, East Sussex, BN23 6NW, UK. Used by permission.

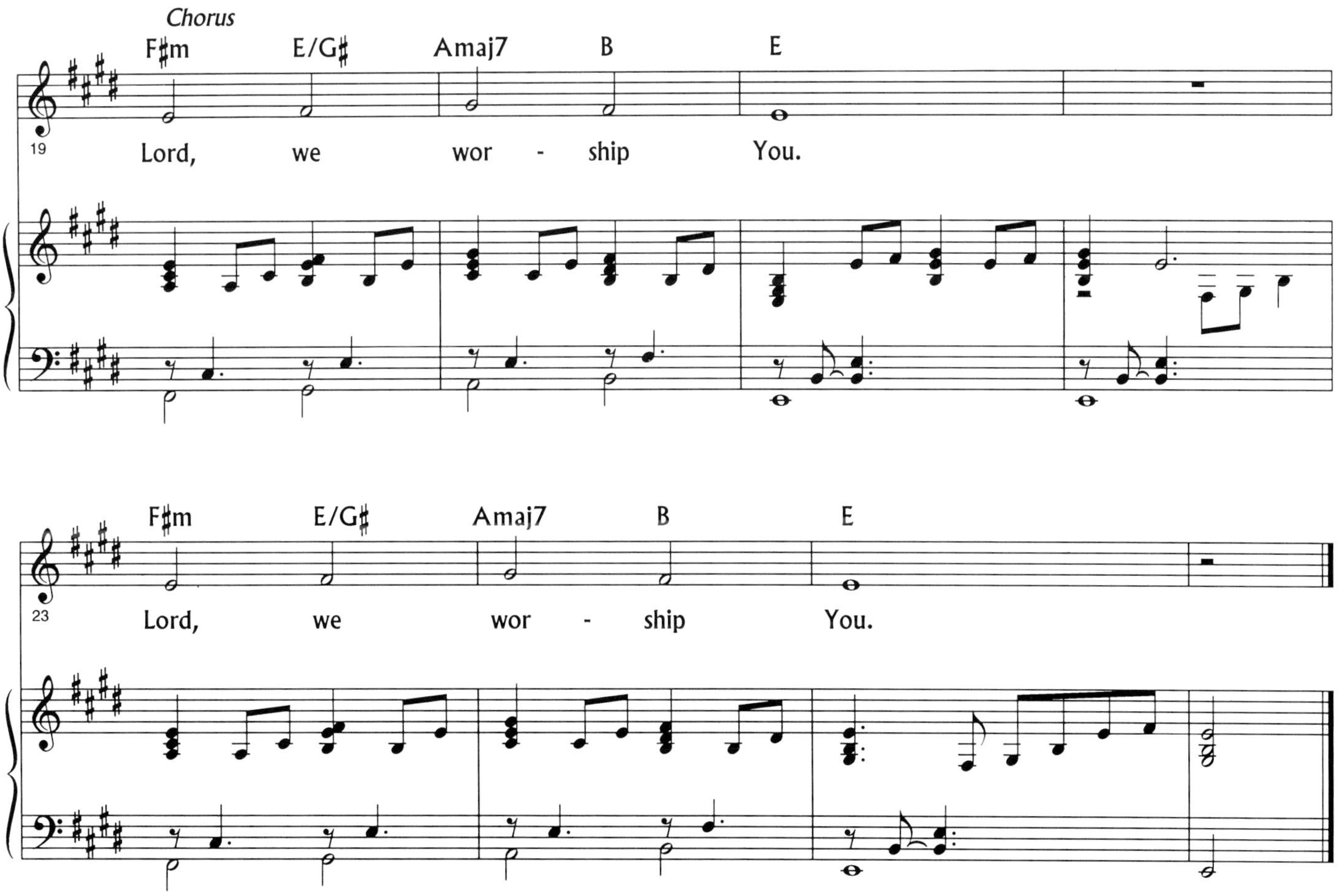
Chorus
F♯m E/G♯ Amaj7 B E
19
Lord, we wor - ship You.
F♯m E/G♯ Amaj7 B E
23
Lord, we wor - ship You.

LET ALL THE WORLD

George Herbert

1. Let all the world in ev'ry corner sing: My God and King! The heav'ns are not too high, His praise may thither fly. The earth is not too low, His praises there may grow. Let all the world in ev'ry corner sing: My God and King!

2. Let all the world in ev'ry corner sing: My God and King! The church with psalms must shout no door can keep them out. But above all the heart must bear the longest part. Let all the world in ev'ry corner sing: My God and King!

Public Domain

WE WORSHIP AND ADORE YOU

words and music: Andy Piercy
(verse 4 lyrics: Cecil Frances Alexander)

1. We worship and adore You, Lord, hear us when we call, for there is no god above You, You are the Lord of all.
2. But how can we begin to express what's on our hearts? There are not words enough, Lord, for us to even start.
3. The tongues of men and angels, we need, to sing your praise, so that we may glorify Your name through heav'n's eternal days.

4. There was no other

Copyright © 1994 IQ Music Limited,
Orchard House, Broad Street, Tylers Green, Cuckfield, West Sussex, RH17 5DZ, UK. Used by permission.

C F B♭ C F B♭ C
12
good e-nough to pay the price of sin; You on-ly could un-lock
F B♭ C F F B♭ C
16
the gate of heav'n and let us in. 1. So we wor - ship and a-dore
F B♭ C F B♭ C
20
You, Lord, hear us when we call, for there is no god a-bove
F B♭ C F
1.
2.
24
You, You are the Lord of all. So we wor -

THE LORD IS MY LIGHT

Jamie Haith

1. The Lord is my light and my salvation, whom shall I fear? The Lord is my strength, the strength of my life, whom shall I dread?

Chorus
One thing I have asked of the Lord,

Copyright © 1997 IQ Music Limited,
Orchard House, Broad Street, Tylers Green, Cuckfield, West Sussex, RH17 5DZ, UK. Used by permission.

that I shall seek, that I may dwell in Your house all my days, That I may gaze on your beau-ty Oh Lord.

2. I would have despaired un-

less I be-lieved that I would see your good-ness; so I will wait, and I will be strong, yes I will wait for You.

MY JESUS, MY SAVIOUR

Darlene Zschech

My Jesus, my Saviour, Lord, there is none like you. All of my days, I want to praise the wonders of your mighty love.

My comfort, my shelter, tower of refuge and strength. Let every breath, all that I am, never cease to worship you.

Copyright © 1993 Darlene Zschech/Hillsongs Australia. Administered by Kingsway's Thankyou Music,
P.O. Box 75, Eastbourne, East Sussex, BN23 6NW, UK. Used by permission.

Chorus

Shout to the Lord, all the earth, let us sing: power and ma-jes-ty, praise to the King,

moun-tains bow down and the seas will roar at the sound of your name.

I sing for joy at the work of your hands. For-ev-er I'll love you, for-ev-er I'll stand,

no-thing com-pares to the prom-ise I have in you.

OUR FATHER

Simon Dixon

Our Father who art in heaven hallowed be Thy name.

Thy kingdom come, Thy will be done on earth as in heaven.

Give us this day our daily bread, and forgive our sins,

as we forgive those who sin against us. Lead us not into temp-

Copyright © 1997 IQ Music Limited,
Orchard House, Broad Street, Tylers Green, Cuckfield, West Sussex, RH17 5DZ, UK. Used by permission.

Em F Gsus4 G E/G♯ Am Em
18 ta - tion, but de - li - ver us from ev - il. For Thine is the king - dom, and the
F Gsus4 G E/G♯ Am Em F
23 pow - er and the glo - ry for ev - er and ev - er a -
Gsus4 G E/G♯ Am Em F Gsus4 G
28 men; for ev - er and ev - er a - men.
C G C F
33
C G F C
37

I WILL OFFER UP MY LIFE

Matt Redman

1. I will offer up my life in spirit and truth, pouring out the oil of love as my worship to You. In surrender I must give my ev'ry part; Lord, receive the sacrifice of a broken heart.

2. You deserve my ev'ry breath for You've paid the great cost; giving up Your life to death, even death on a cross. You took all my shame away, there defeated my sin, opened up the gates of heav'n, and have beckoned me in.

Chorus
Jesus what can I give, what can I bring to so faithful a friend,

Copyright © 1994 Kingsway's Thankyou Music,
P.O. Box 75, Eastbourne, East Sussex, BN23 6NW, UK. Used by permission.

to so lov-ing a King? Sa-viour, what can be said, what can be sung as a praise of Your name for the things You have done? O, my words could not tell, not ev-en in part, of the debt of love that is owed by this thank-ful heart.

JESUS CHRIST

Matt Redman

1. Jesus Christ, I think upon Your sacrifice; You became nothing, poured out to death. Many times I've wondered at Your gift of life, and I'm in that place once again,
2. Now You are exalted to the highest place, King of the heavens, where one day I'll bow. But for now I marvel at this saving grace, and I'm full of praise once again,

I'm in that place once again.
I'm full of praise once again.

Chorus
And once again I look upon the cross where You died. I'm

Copyright © 1996 Kingsway's Thankyou Music,
P.O. Box 75, Eastbourne, East Sussex, BN23 6NW, UK. Used by permission.

humbled by Your mercy and I'm broken inside. Once again I thank You once again I pour out my life.

IN MY LIFE, LORD

Bob Kilpatrick

In my life, Lord, be glorified, be glorified. In my life, Lord, be glorified today.

Copyright © 1978 Bob Kilpatrick Music. Administered by CopyCare,
P.O. Box 77, Hailsham, East Sussex, BN27 3EF, UK. Used by permission.

RAIN AND SNOW FALL FROM THE SKY

Jamie Haith

Rain and snow fall from the sky, pouring down upon the earth, causing it to spring to life, making new things come to birth. And so is Your word, our Lord, it does not return to You having not achieved Your will; doing all You want it to. We will call on You while You are near. We will seek You while You may be found. (So) Rain

Copyright © 1997 IQ Music Limited,
Orchard House, Broad Street, Tylers Green, Cuckfield, West Sussex, RH17 5DZ, UK. Used by permission.

down, (rain down,) rain down, (rain down,) pour the wa-ter of Your Spi-rit on this dry _ and thirs-ty ground. _ Rain down, (rain down,) rain down, (rain down,) speak Your word in-to our deaf-ness. Bring Your heal-ing to our land. _ Rain

1. heal-ing to our land: _ rain _ down.

2. heal-ing to our land: _ rain _ down.

HERE WE STAND

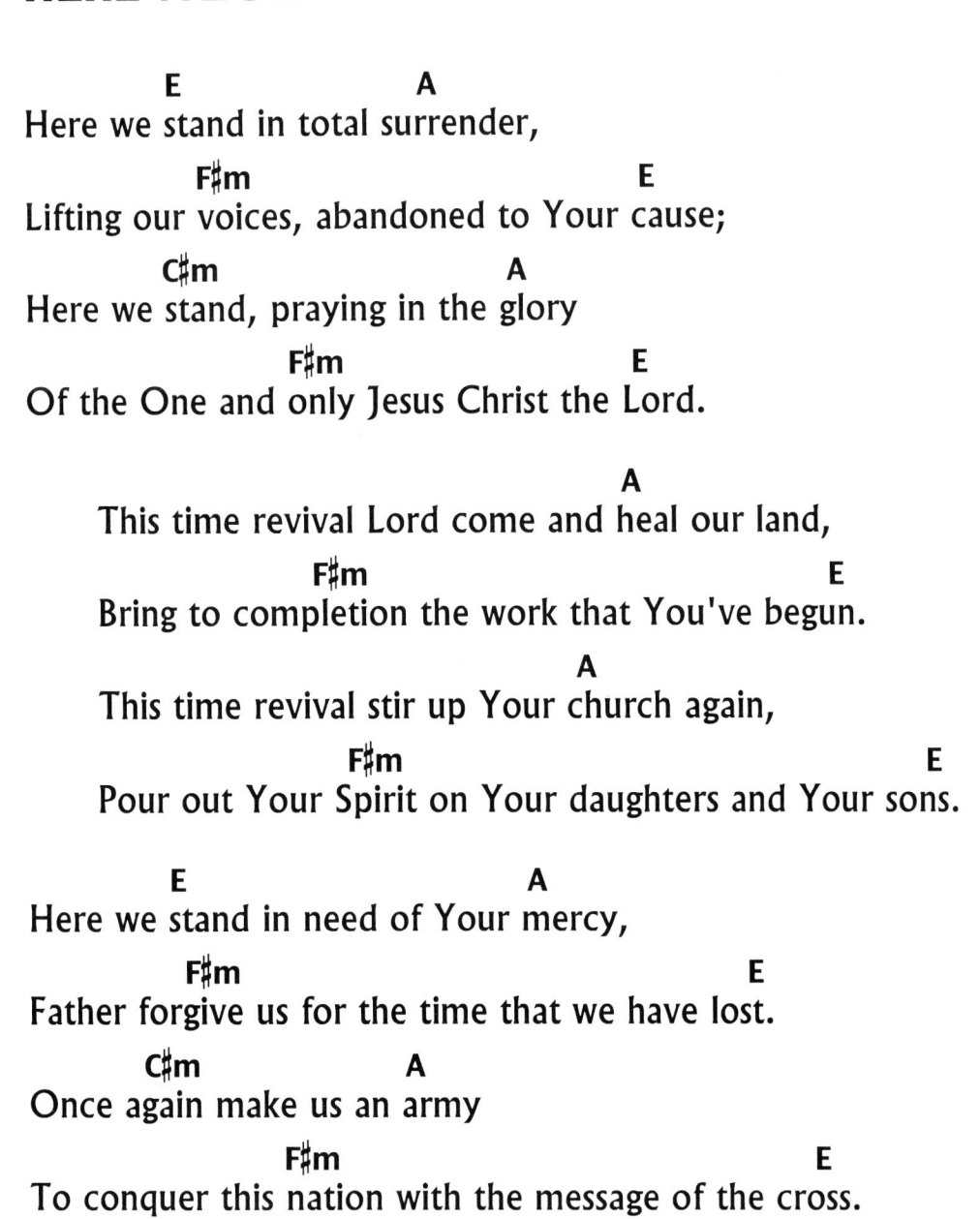

        E   A
Here we stand in total surrender,
       F♯m   E
Lifting our voices, abandoned to Your cause;
     C♯m   A
Here we stand, praying in the glory
        F♯m   E
Of the One and only Jesus Christ the Lord.

                          A
This time revival Lord come and heal our land,
       F♯m   E
Bring to completion the work that You've begun.
                    A
This time revival stir up Your church again,
       F♯m   E
Pour out Your Spirit on Your daughters and Your sons.

       E   A
Here we stand in need of Your mercy,
       F♯m   E
Father forgive us for the time that we have lost.
     C♯m   A
Once again make us an army
        F♯m   E
To conquer this nation with the message of the cross.

CHORDS USED IN THIS SONG

E   A   F♯   C♯m

A. Piercy & C. Groves
Copyright © 1995 IQ Music Limited
Orchard House, Broad Street, Tylers Green, Cuckfield, West Sussex, RH17 5DZ, UK
Used by permission.

HERE WE STAND

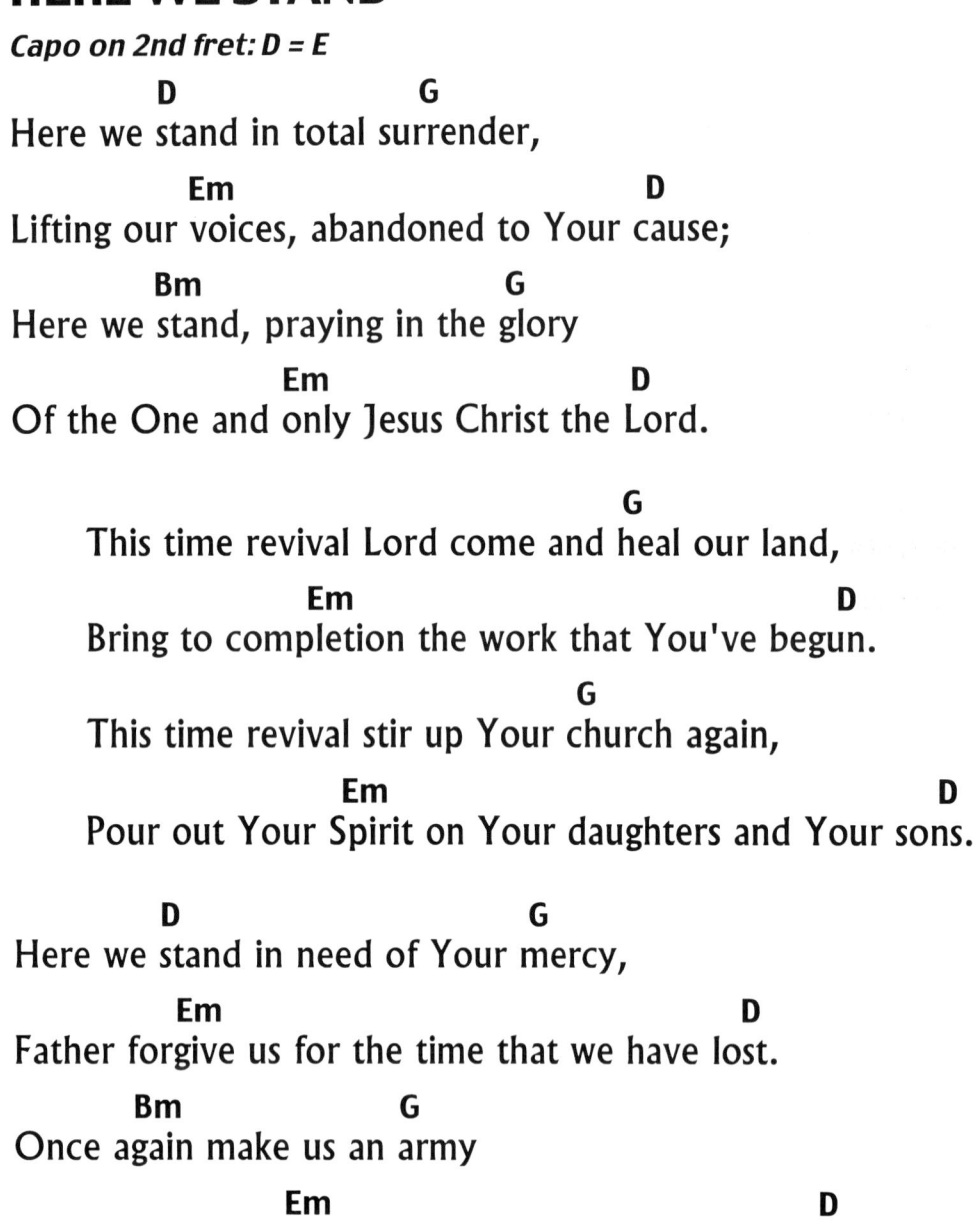

Capo on 2nd fret: D = E

```
        D                G
Here we stand in total surrender,
       Em                      D
Lifting our voices, abandoned to Your cause;
      Bm              G
Here we stand, praying in the glory
           Em                  D
Of the One and only Jesus Christ the Lord.

                                  G
        This time revival Lord come and heal our land,
             Em                           D
        Bring to completion the work that You've begun.
                                 G
        This time revival stir up Your church again,
             Em                                      D
        Pour out Your Spirit on Your daughters and Your sons.

        D                    G
Here we stand in need of Your mercy,
       Em                              D
Father forgive us for the time that we have lost.
       Bm              G
Once again make us an army
            Em                                    D
To conquer this nation with the message of the cross.
```

CHORD SHAPES USED IN THIS SONG (capo on 2nd fret)

D   G   Em   Bm

A. Piercy & C. Groves
Copyright © 1995 IQ Music Limited
Orchard House, Broad Street, Tylers Green, Cuckfield, West Sussex, RH17 5DZ, UK
Used by permission.

LORD, YOU ARE CALLING

Em   D
  Lord, You are calling the people of Your Kingdom
     C   D   Em
  To battle in Your name against the enemy.
                 D
  To stand before You a people who will serve You,
     C   D   Bsus4 B
  'Til Your Kingdom is released throughout the earth

       G   C   D   Em   C
    Let Your Kingdom come let Your will be done
    Am   Am/G   Dsus4 D
  On earth as it is in heaven.
       G   C   D   Em   C
    Let Your Kingdom come let Your will be done
    Am   Am/G   Dsus4 D
  On earth as it is in heaven.

Em   D
  At the name of Jesus every knee must bow;
     C   D   Em
  The darkness of this age must flee away.
                 D
  Release Your power to flow throughout the land,
     C   D   Bsus4 B
  Let Your glory be revealed as we praise.

CHORDS USED IN THIS SONG

Em   D   C   Bsus4   B   G   Am/G   Dsus4   Am

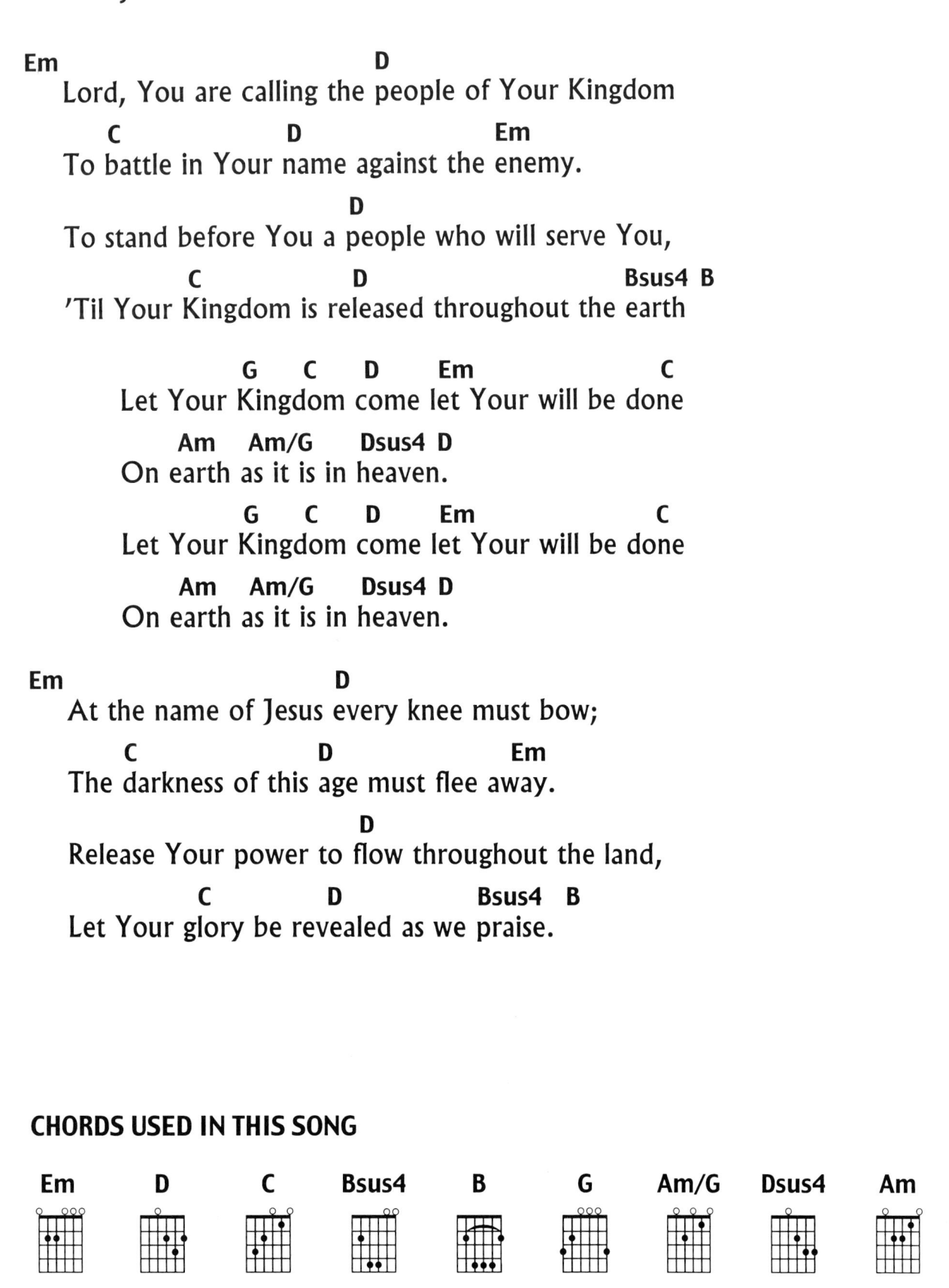

Simon & Lorraine Fenner
Copyright © 1989 Kingsway's Thankyou Music
P.O. Box 75, Eastbourne, East Sussex, BN23 6NW, UK
Used by permission.

BREATHE ON ME, BREATH OF GOD

    D G A D
Breathe on me, breath of God,
  G   D/F♯ G Asus4 A
Fill me with life anew,
    D Em D/F♯ G A Bm G Asus4 A   D
That I may love what Thou dost love and do what Thou wouldst do.

    D G A D
Breathe on me, breath of God,
  G   D/F♯ G Asus4 A
Until my heart is pure:
   D Em D/F♯ G A Bm G Asus4 A D
Until my will is one with Thine, to do and to endure.

    D G A D
Breathe on me, breath of God,
   G D/F♯ G Asus4 A
Till I am wholly Thine,
   D Em D/F♯ G A Bm G Asus4 A D
Until this earthly part of me glows with Thy fire divine.

    D G A D
Breathe on me, breath of God,
   G D/F♯ G Asus4 A
So shall I never die,
    D Em   D/F♯ G A Bm G Asus4 A D
But live with Thee the perfect life of Thine eternity.

CHORDS USED IN THIS SONG

Em D C Asus4 B G Am/G Dsus4 D/F♯

E. Hatch (1878)
Public Domain

BY HIS GRACE

```
D         G   A D
By His grace I am redeemed,

D/F#     G   A   D
By His blood I am made clean,

D/F#        G   A   Bm  Em7 A
And I now can know Him face to face.

D/F#        G   A   D
By His power I have been raised,

D/F#       G   A   D
Hidden now in Christ by faith.

D/F#         G  A  G/B A/C# D
I will praise the glory of His grace.
```

CHORDS USED IN THIS SONG

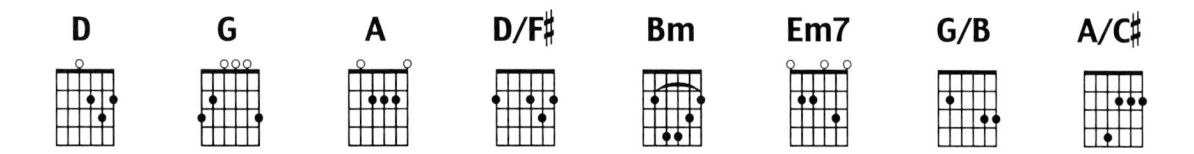

D G A D/F# Bm Em7 G/B A/C#

Steve Fry
Copyright © 1994 Deep Fryed Music. Administered by CopyCare
P.O. Box 77, Hailsham, East Sussex, BN23 3EF, UK
Used by permission.

FAITHFUL ONE

```
    D              Em
Faithful One, so unchanging,
    A            G       D
Ageless One, You're my rock of peace.
    Bm    Bm/A  Em
Lord of all, I depend on You,
A       D G A          D G A
I call out to You    again and again,
        D G A         D  Dsus
I call out to You    again and again.
D          A    G       D
You are my rock in times of trouble,
         A  G        D
You lift me up   when I fall down.
       A    D   G    D/F# G    D/F# G
All through the storm Your love is the anchor,
   D/F# G  Bm/A A7    D
My hope is in    You alone.
```

CHORDS USED IN THIS SONG

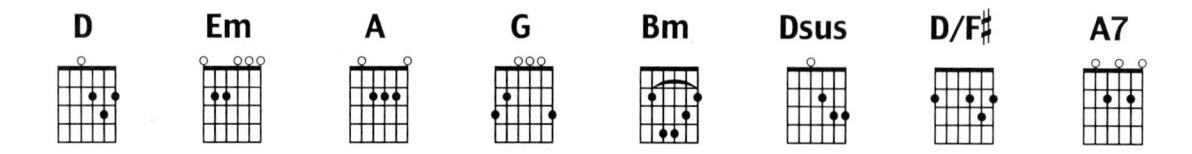

D   Em   A   G   Bm   Dsus   D/F#   A7

Brian Doerksen
Copyright © 1987 Mercy Publishing/Kingsway's Thankyou Music
P.O. Box 75, Eastbourne, East Sussex, BN23 6NW, UK
Used by permission.

I WILL WORSHIP

```
G                      F
I will worship (echo) with all of my heart (echo)
C                 G              Am7    D
I will praise You (echo) with all of my strength (all my strength)
G                    F
I will seek You (echo) all of my days (echo)
C                G              Am7    D
I will follow (echo) all of Your ways (all Your ways)
```

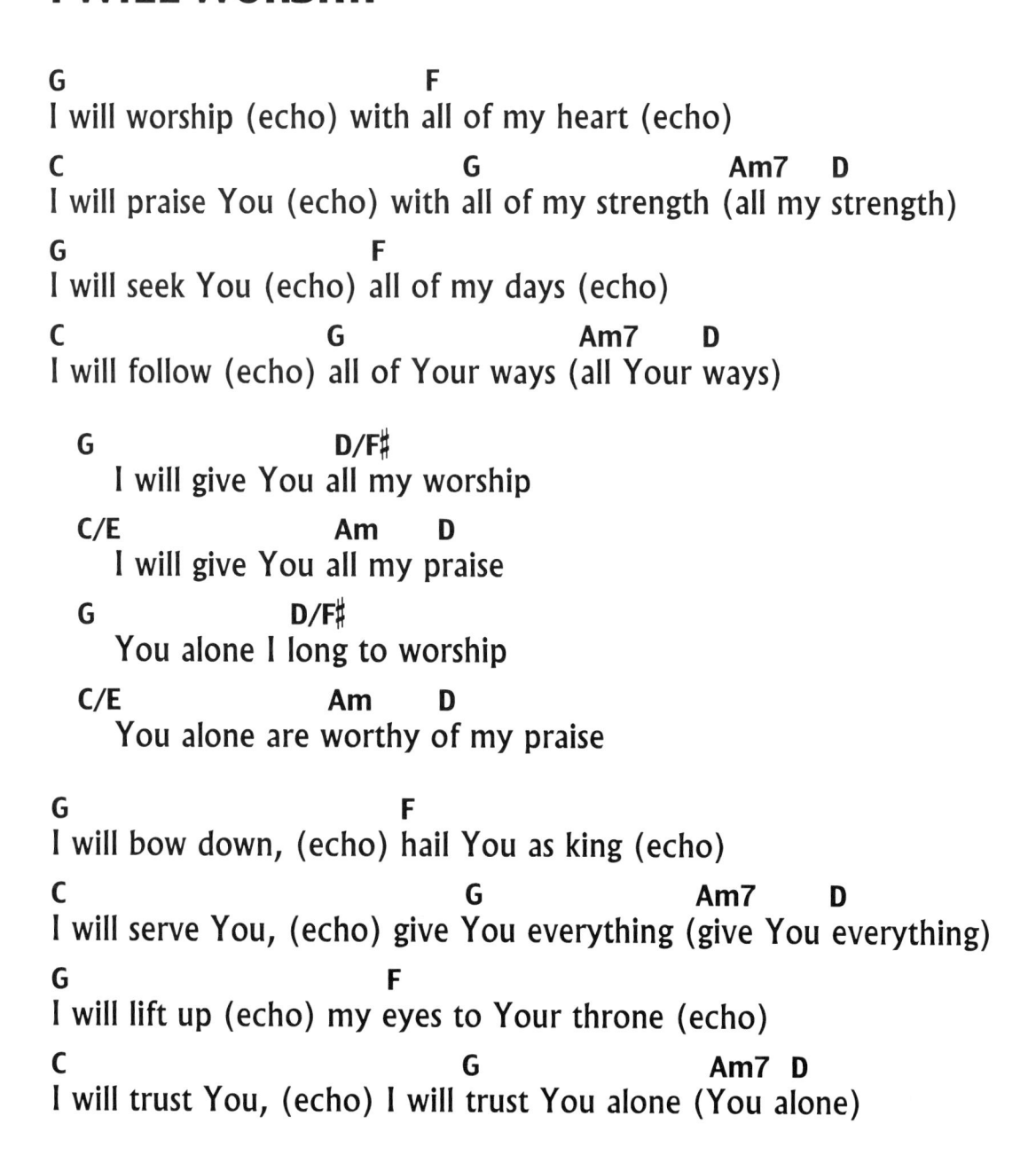

```
   G              D/F#
   I will give You all my worship
   C/E          Am     D
   I will give You all my praise
   G              D/F#
   You alone I long to worship
   C/E          Am       D
   You alone are worthy of my praise
```

```
G                    F
I will bow down, (echo) hail You as king (echo)
C                    G              Am7    D
I will serve You, (echo) give You everything (give You everything)
G                  F
I will lift up (echo) my eyes to Your throne (echo)
C                   G              Am7   D
I will trust You, (echo) I will trust You alone (You alone)
```

CHORDS USED IN THIS SONG

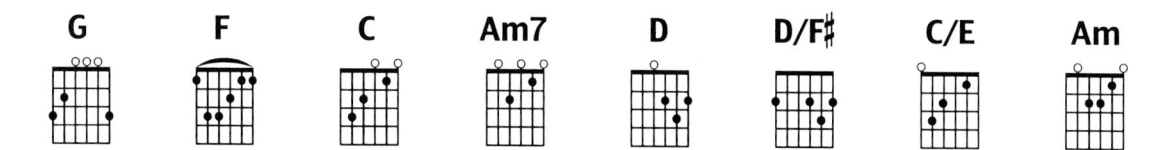

G   F   C   Am7   D   D/F#   C/E   Am

David Ruis
Copyright © 1993 Shade Tree Music/Maranatha! Music. Administered by Kingsway's Thankyou Music
P.O. Box 75, Eastbourne, East Sussex, BN23 6NW, UK
Used by permission.

OVERWHELMED BY LOVE

G D/F♯ C   G
Overwhelmed by love,
C   G   C   Em D/F♯
Deeper than oceans, high as the heavens.
G D/F♯ C D G
Ev-er   living God,
C   Dsus4 D G
Your love has rescued me.

   D/F♯ C   G
All my sin was laid
C   G   C   Em D/F♯
On Your dear Son, Your precious One.
G D/F♯ C   D G
All my debt He paid,
C   Dsus4 D G
Great is Your love for me.

   G   Am G/B   C   G
No one could ever earn Your love,
Am   Am/G   D
Your grace and mercy is free.
G   D/F♯ C   D   G
Lord, these words are true,
C   Dsus4 D Em
So is my love for You,
C   Dsus4 D G
So is my love for You.

CHORDS USED IN THIS SONG

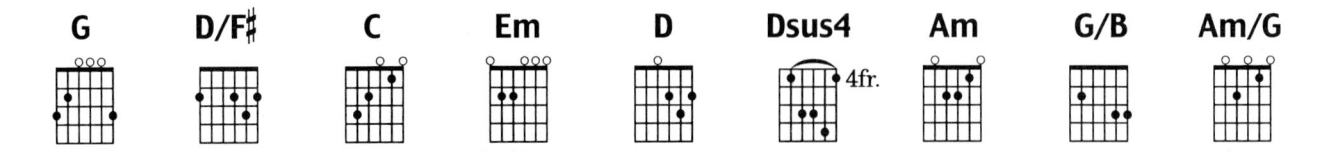

G   D/F♯   C   Em   D   Dsus4 (4fr.)   Am   G/B   Am/G

Noel Richards
Copyright © 1994 Kingsway's Thankyou Music
P.O. Box 75, Eastbourne, East Sussex, BN23 6NW, UK
Used by permission.

FATHER GOD, FILL THIS PLACE

Capo on 2nd fret: D = E

G/B A/C♯ D   Bm G A
Fa - ther God, fill this place

G/B A/C♯ D   Bm G   A
With Your love, with Your grace.

      Gmaj7 A   Bm Bm/A
As we call on Your name,

   G Em7   D
Visit us in power again.

G/B A/C♯ D   Bm G   A
Spi - rit come with Your peace,

G/B A/C♯ D   Bm G A
Heal our   wounds, bring release.

      Gmaj7   A   Bm Bm/A
Lord, we long for Your touch,

   G   Em7 D
Fill our hearts with Your love.

  Em   D/F♯ Gmaj7 A   D
Lord, we wor - ship You.

  Em   D/F♯ Gmaj7 A   D
Lord, we wor - ship You.

CHORD SHAPES USED IN THIS SONG

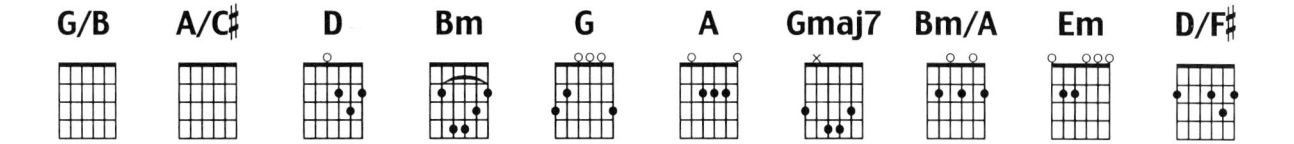

G/B A/C♯ D Bm G A Gmaj7 Bm/A Em D/F♯

Dave Bilbrough
Copyright © 1995 Kingsway's Thankyou Music
P.O. Box 75, Eastbourne, East Sussex, BN23 6NW, UK
Used by permission.

FATHER GOD, FILL THIS PLACE

```
A/C#  B/D# E      C#m A  B
Fa - ther  God, fill this place
A/C#  B/D# E      C#m A  B
With Your love, with Your grace.
         Amaj7  B    C#m  C#m/B
As we call on Your name,
      A  F#m7      E
Visit us   in power again.

A/C#  B/D# E      C#m A  B
Spi - rit  come with Your peace,
A/C#  B/D# E      C#m A B
Heal our   wounds, bring release.
         Amaj7   B    C#m  C#m/B
Lord, we long for Your touch,
      A   F#m7      E
Fill our hearts with Your love.

    F#m   E/G# Amaj7 B    E
Lord, we  wor - ship You.
    F#m   E/G# Amaj7 B    E
Lord, we  wor - ship You.
```

CHORDS USED IN THIS SONG

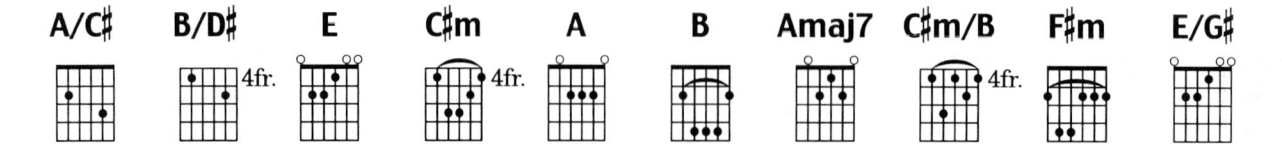

A/C#   B/D#   E   C#m   A   B   Amaj7   C#m/B   F#m   E/G#

Dave Bilbrough
Copyright © 1995 Kingsway's Thankyou Music
P.O. Box 75, Eastbourne, East Sussex, BN23 6NW, UK
Used by permission.

LET ALL THE WORLD

```
      D  A/C# Bm       Em/G Em A  A7 D
Let all the  world in ev - 'ry corner sing:

A/C# Bm/D E   A
My God   and King!

D/F# G       Em7 A      D   D/F# G      Em7 A      D
The heavens are not too high, His praise may thither fly.

A/C# D   Bm7 Esus4 E   A    A/C# D Bm7 Esus4 E    A
The earth is   not  too low, His praises there may grow.

      D  A/C# Bm       Em/G Em A  A7 D
Let all the  world in ev - 'ry corner sing:

D/F# Em/G A   D
My  God  and King!


      D  A/C# Bm       Em/G Em A  A7 D
Let all the  world in ev - 'ry corner sing:

A/C# Bm/D E   A
My God   and King!

D/F# G       Em7 A       D   D/F# G      Em7 A      D
The church with psalms must shout no door can keep them out.

A/C# D  Bm7 Esus4 E   A     A/C# D    Bm7 Esus4 E    A
But a - bove all   the heart must bear the long - est part.

      D  A/C# Bm       Em/G Em A  A7 D
Let all the  world in ev - 'ry corner sing:

D/F# Em/G A   D
My  God  and King!
```

CHORDS USED IN THIS SONG

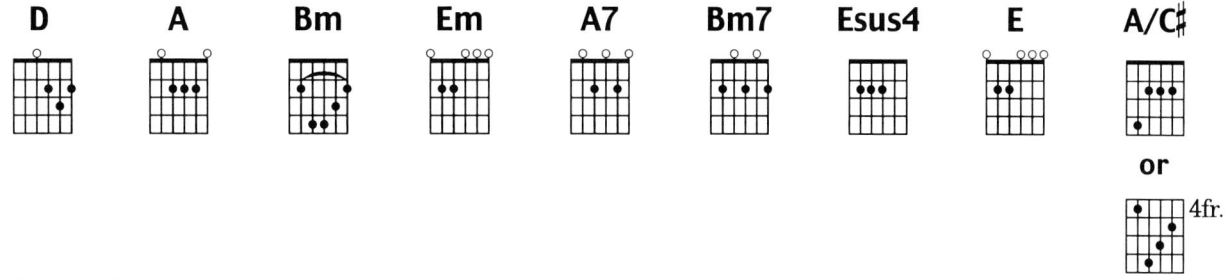

D A Bm Em A7 Bm7 Esus4 E A/C#

or 4fr.

George Herbert
Public Domain

WE WORSHIP AND ADORE YOU

```
     F     Bb   C   F        Bb                  C
We worship and adore You, Lord, hear us when we call,
        F    Bb   C   F       Bb     C     F
For there is no God above You, You are the Lord of all.

     F        Bb    C   F   Bb                 C
But how can we begin to express what's on our hearts?
       F      Bb   C    F      Bb    C    F
There are not words enough, Lord, for us to even start.

       F         Bb     C  F     Bb               C
The tongues of men and angels, we need, to sing your praise,
        F      Bb  C      F          Bb      C    F
So that we may glorify Your name through heaven's eternal days.

       Dm         C    F      Bb               C
There was no other good enough to pay the price of sin;
      F    Bb    C     F      Bb     C     F
You only could unlock the gate of heaven and let us in.
```

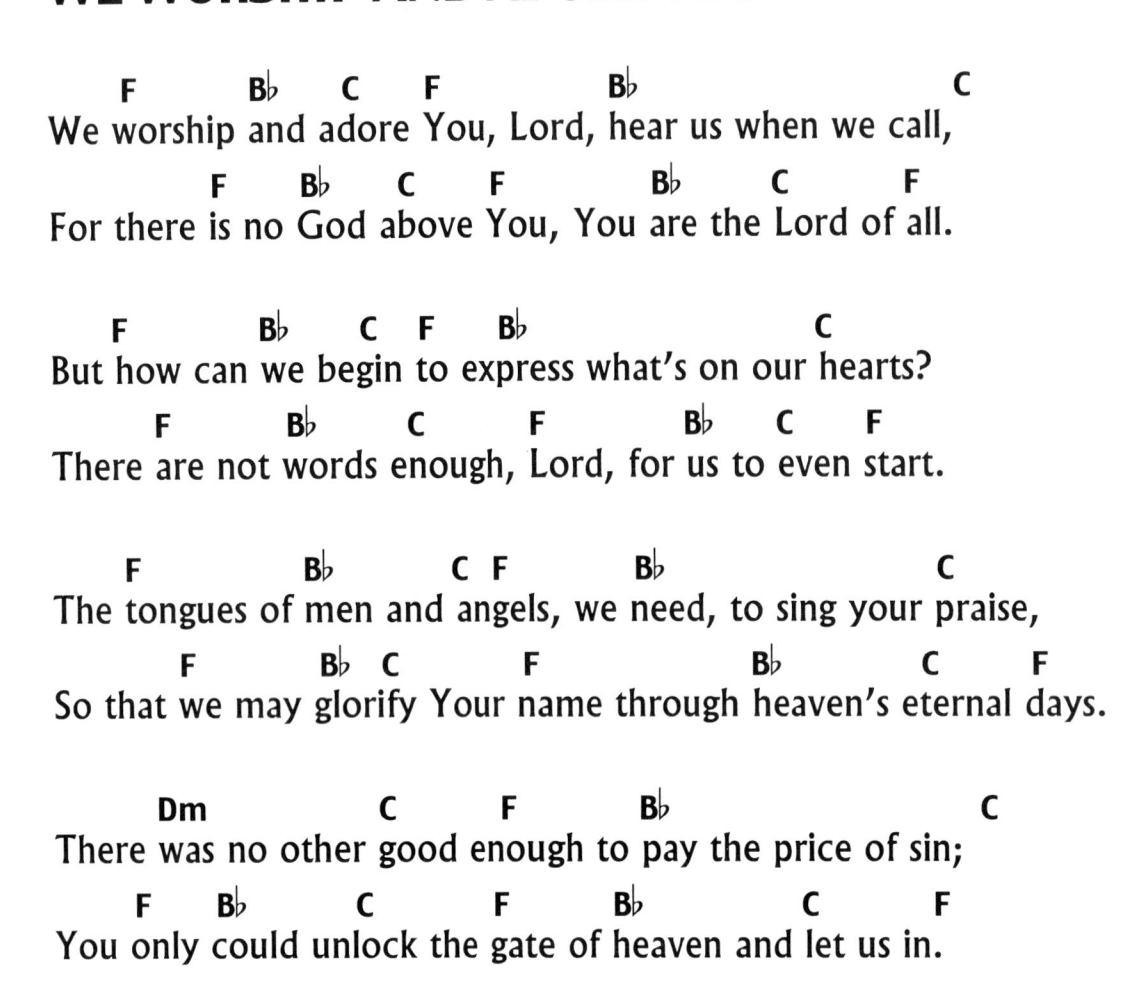

CHORDS USED IN THIS SONG

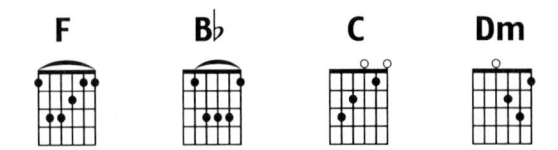

F   Bb   C   Dm

A. Piercy
Copyright © 1995 IQ Music Limited
Orchard House, Broad Street, Tylers Green, Cuckfield, West Sussex, RH17 5DZ, UK
Used by permission.

WE WORSHIP AND ADORE YOU

Capo on 3rd fret: D = F

```
    D     G    A    D    G              A
We worship and adore You, Lord, hear us when we call,
    D     G    A    D        G    A    D
For there is no God above You, You are the Lord of all.


    D     G    A  D    G              A
But how can we begin to express what's on our hearts?
    D     G    A    D        G    A    D
There are not words enough, Lord, for us to even start.


    D        G    A D      G              A
The tongues of men and angels, we need, to sing your praise,
    D     G    A    D           G    A    D
So that we may glorify Your name through heaven's eternal days.


       Bm        A     D     G              A
There was no other good enough to pay the price of sin;
    D  G    A     D       G      A    D
You only could unlock the gate of heaven and let us in.
```

CHORD SHAPES USED IN THIS SONG

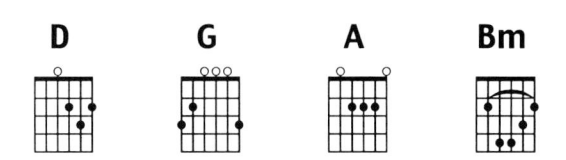

D   G   A   Bm

A. Piercy
Copyright © 1995 IQ Music Limited
Orchard House, Broad Street, Tylers Green, Cuckfield, West Sussex, RH17 5DZ, UK
Used by permission.

THE LORD IS MY LIGHT

Bb   F   Bb F   Bb
The Lord is my light and my salvation,

F   Bb   Gm F
Whom shall I fear?

F   Bb   F   Bb
The Lord is my strength, the strength of my life,

F   Bb   Gm F
Whom shall I dread?

Cm   Gm   F
One thing I have asked of the Lord,

Cm   Gm
That I shall seek,

Cm   Gm   F   Eb
That I may dwell in Your house all my days,

Gm   F   Eb
That I may gaze on your beauty Oh Lord.

Bb F   Bb F   Bb
I would have despaired unless I believed

F   Bb   Gm F
That I would see your goodness;

F   Bb F   Bb
So I will wait, and I will be strong,

F   Bb   Gm F
Yes I will wait for You.

CHORDS USED IN THIS SONG

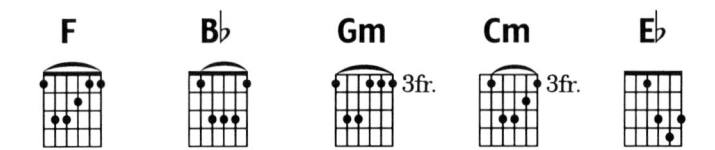

F   Bb   Gm 3fr.   Cm 3fr.   Eb

Jamie Haith
Copyright © 1997 IQ Music Limited
Orchard House, Broad Street, Tylers Green, Cuckfield, West Sussex, RH17 5DZ, UK
Used by permission.

THE LORD IS MY LIGHT

Capo on 3rd fret: G = Bb

G   D   G   D   G
The Lord is my light and my salvation,

D   G   Em D
Whom shall I fear?

        D   G   D   G
The Lord is my strength, the strength of my life,

D   G   Em G
Whom shall I dread?

    Am   Em   D
One thing I have asked of the Lord,

    Am   Em
That I shall seek,

    Am   Em   D   C
That I may dwell in Your house all my days,

       Em   D   C
That I may gaze on your beauty Oh Lord.

G D   G   D   G
I would have despaired unless I believed

D   G   Em D
That I would see your goodness;

D   G D   G
So I will wait, and I will be strong,

D   G   Em D
Yes I will wait for You.

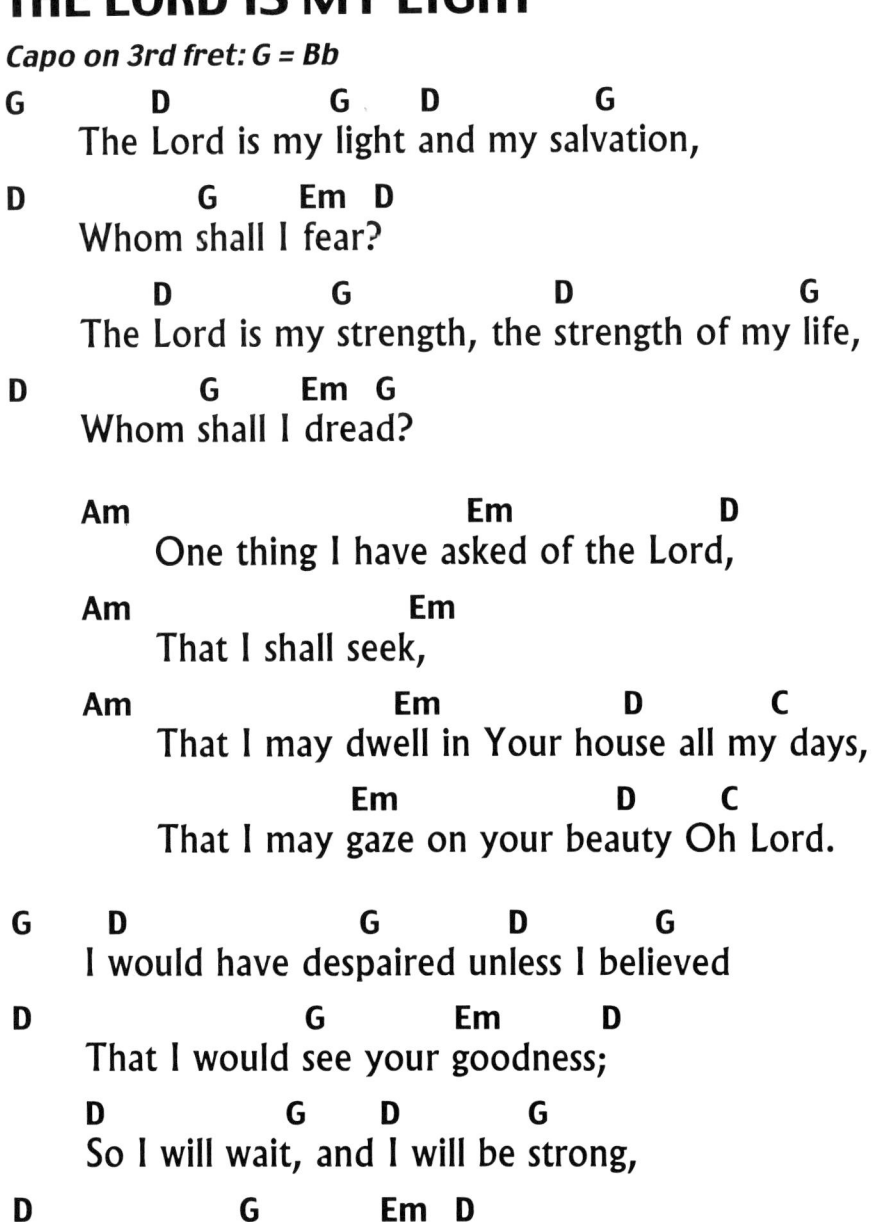

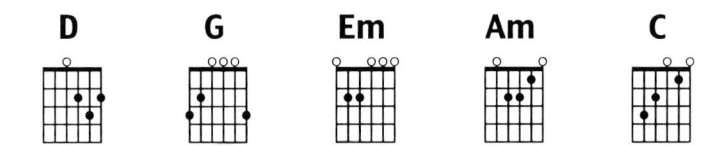

CHORD SHAPES USED IN THIS SONG

D   G   Em   Am   C

Jamie Haith
Copyright © 1997 IQ Music Limited
Orchard House, Broad Street, Tylers Green, Cuckfield, West Sussex, RH17 5DZ, UK
Used by permission.

MY JESUS, MY SAVIOUR

Bb   F
My Jesus, my Saviour,
Gm   F   Eb
Lord, there is none like you.
                Bb/D Eb   Bb/F   Gm7   Ab Eb/G Fsus4 F
All of my days   I want to praise the wonders of Your mighty love.
Bb   F
My comfort, my shelter,
Gm   F   Eb
Tower of refuge and strength.
                Bb/D Eb   Bb/F Gm   Ab Eb/G Fsus4 F
Let every breath, all that I am, never cease to worship You.

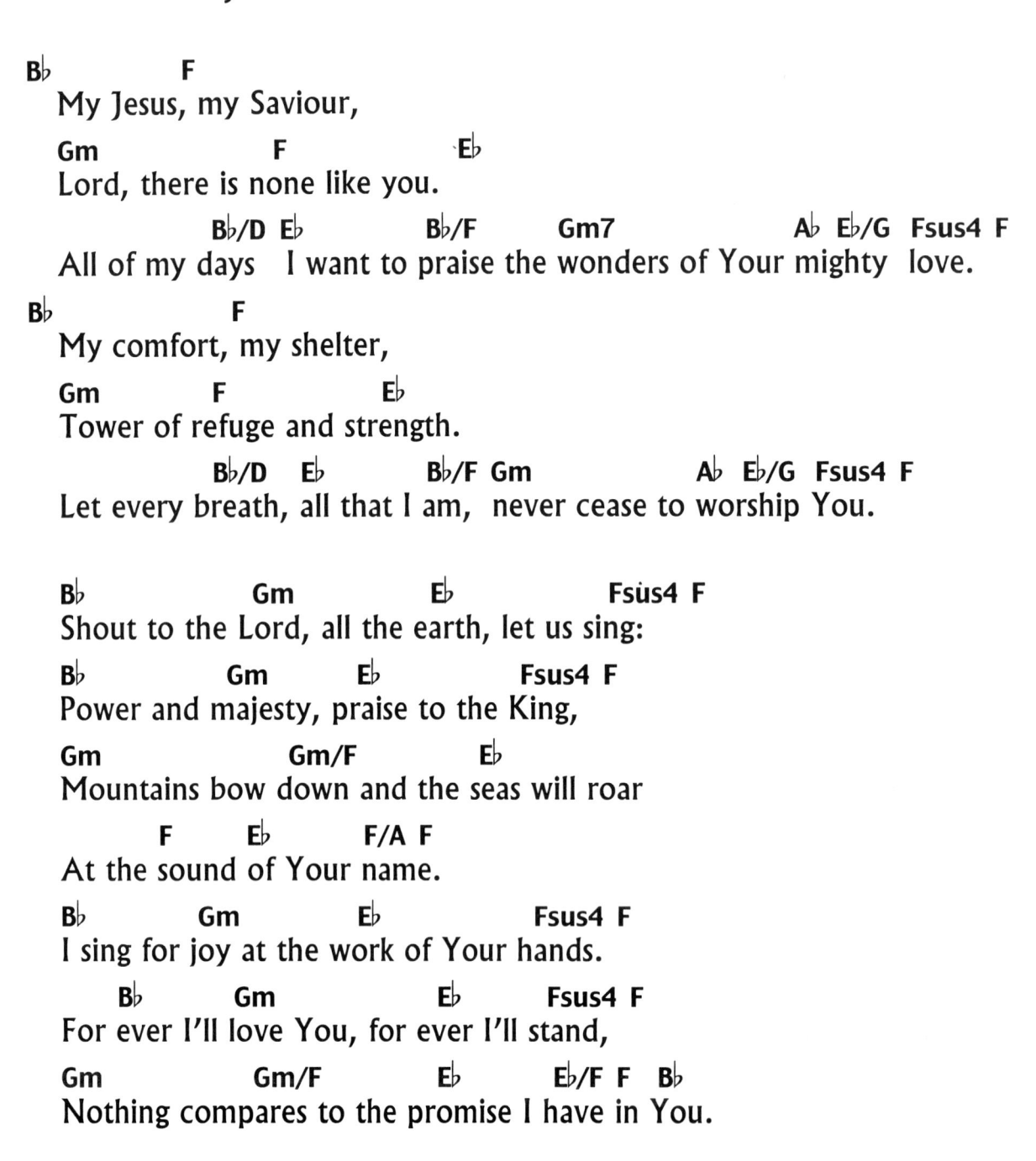

Bb   Gm   Eb   Fsus4 F
Shout to the Lord, all the earth, let us sing:
Bb   Gm   Eb   Fsus4 F
Power and majesty, praise to the King,
Gm   Gm/F   Eb
Mountains bow down and the seas will roar
        F   Eb   F/A F
At the sound of Your name.
Bb   Gm   Eb   Fsus4 F
I sing for joy at the work of Your hands.
   Bb   Gm   Eb   Fsus4 F
For ever I'll love You, for ever I'll stand,
Gm   Gm/F   Eb   Eb/F F Bb
Nothing compares to the promise I have in You.

CHORDS USED IN THIS SONG

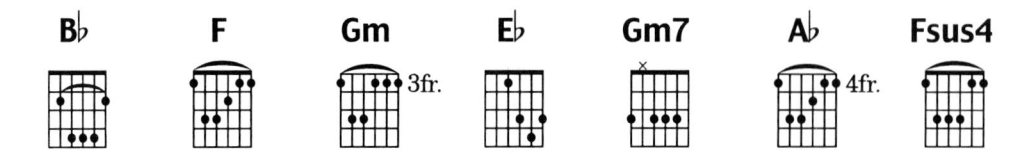

Bb   F   Gm   Eb   Gm7   Ab   Fsus4

Darlene Zschech
Copyright © 1993 Darlene Zschech/Hillsongs Australia. Administered by Kingsway's Thankyou Music
P.O. Box 75, Eastbourne, East Sussex, BN23 6NW, UK
Used by permission.

MY JESUS, MY SAVIOUR

Capo on 3rd fret: G = Bb

G	D
My Jesus, my Saviour,

| Em | D | C |
Lord, there is none like you.

| | G/B C | G/D | Em7 | F C/E Dsus4 D |
All of my days   I want to praise the wonders of Your mighty love.

| G | D |
My Comfort, my Shelter,

| Em | D | C |
Tower of refuge and strength.

| | G/B C | G/D Em | | F C/E Dsus4 D |
Let every breath, all that I am, never cease to worship You.

| G | Em | C | Dsus4 D |
Shout to the Lord, all the earth, let us sing:

| G | Em | C | Dsus4 D |
Power and majesty, praise to the King,

| Em | Em/D | C |
Mountains bow down and the seas will roar

| | D | C | D/F# | D |
At the sound of Your name.

| G | Em | C | Dsus4 D |
I sing for joy at the work of Your hands.

| | G | Em | C Dsus4 D |
For ever I'll love You, for ever I'll stand,

| Em | Em/D | C | C/D D G |
Nothing compares to the promise I have in You.

CHORD SHAPES USED IN THIS SONG

G   D   Em   C   Em7   F   Dsus4

Darlene Zschech
Copyright © 1993 Darlene Zschech/Hillsongs Australia. Administered by Kingsway's Thankyou Music
P.O. Box 75, Eastbourne, East Sussex, BN23 6NW, UK
Used by permission.

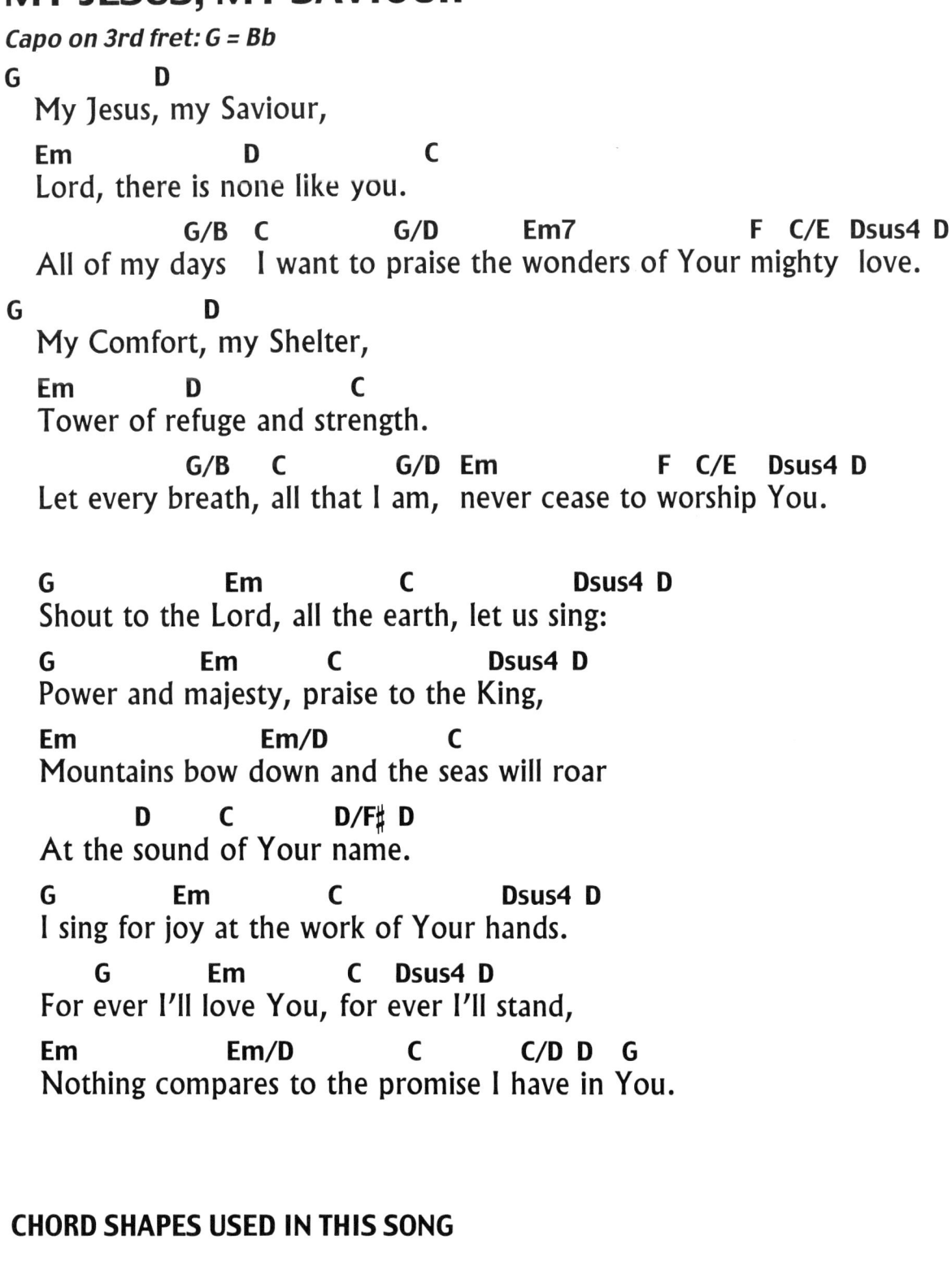

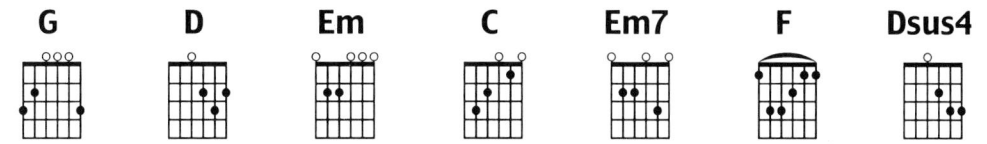

OUR FATHER

C   Gsus   G
Our Father who art in heaven
C   F
Hallowed be Thy name.
C   Gsus   G
Thy kingdom come, Thy will be done
   F   C
On earth as in heaven.
          Gsus   G
Give us this day our daily bread,
C   F
And forgive our sins,
C   Gsus   G F   C
As we forgive those who sin against us.
Am   Em
Lead us not into temptation,
   F   Gsus4 G E/G♯
But deliver us from evil.
Am   Em
For Thine is the kingdom,
   F   Gsus4 G E/G♯
And the power and the glory
Am   Em F Gsus4 G E/G♯
For ever and ever amen;
Am   Em F Gsus4 G C
For ever and ever amen.

(Optional Intro/link: C G C F C G C F)

CHORDS USED IN THIS SONG

C   Gsus   G   F   E/G♯   Am   Em

Simon Dixon
Copyright © 1997 IQ Music Limited
Orchard House, Broad Street, Tylers Green, Cuckfield, West Sussex, RH17 5DZ, UK
Used by permission.

I WILL OFFER UP MY LIFE

```
D      D/F#      G    A         D
  I will offer up my life in spirit and truth,
       D/F#      G    A         D
  Pouring out the oil of love as my worship to You.
       D/F#     G    A      Bm7
  In surrender I must give my every part;
     Bm/A      G      A        D
  Lord, receive the sacrifice of a broken heart.

       D/F#     G    A         D
  Jesus what can I give, what can I bring
       D/F#     G      A       D
  To so faithful a friend, to so loving a King?
       D/F#     G    A         D
  Saviour, what can be said, what can be sung
       D/F#      G      A        D
  As a praise of Your name for the things You have done?
             Em     D/F#     G
  O, my words could not tell, not even in part,
       Em    D/F#    G     A          D
  Of the debt of love that is owed by this thankful heart

D      D/F#      G           A          D
  You deserve my every breath for You've paid the great cost
       D/F#      G       A         D
  Giving up Your life to death, even death on a cross.
       D/F#      G        A         Bm7
  You took all my shame away, there defeated my sin,
      Bm/A      G          A              D
  Opened up the gates of heaven, and have beckoned me in.
```

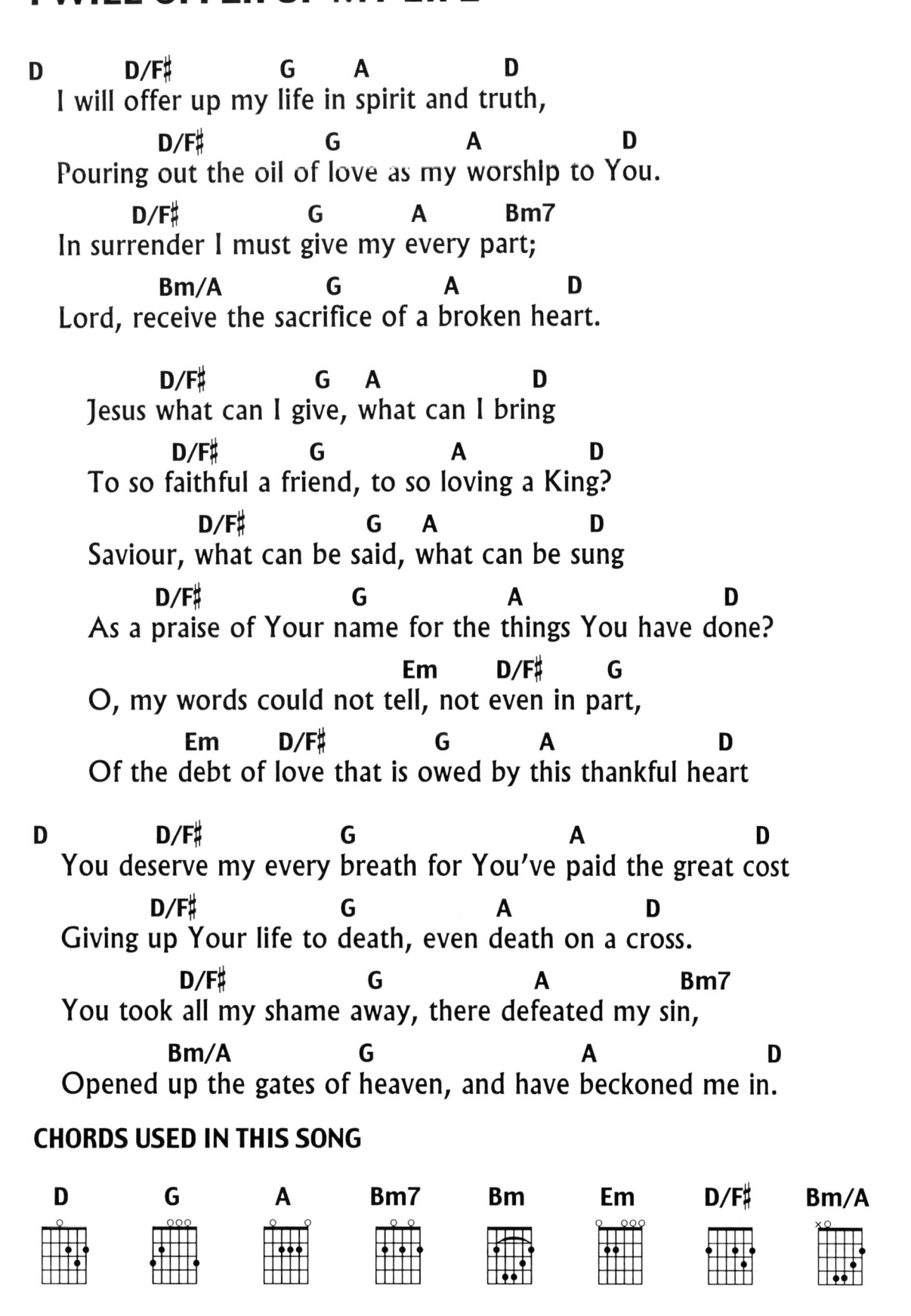

CHORDS USED IN THIS SONG

D   G   A   Bm7   Bm   Em   D/F#   Bm/A

Matt Redman
Copyright © 1994 Kingsway's Thankyou Music
P.O. Box 75, Eastbourne, East Sussex, BN23 6NW, UK
Used by permission.

JESUS CHRIST

D	A/D G		D/F#

Jesus Christ, I think upon Your sacrifice;

Em	D/F# G		A

You became nothing, poured out to death.

D	A/D G		D/F#

Many times I've wondered at Your gift of life,

Em	Asus	D

And I'm in that place once again,

Em	Asus	D

I'm in that place once again.

	D/F#	G	D/F#		A

And once again I look upon the cross where You died.

	D/F#	G	D/F#		A

I'm humbled by Your mercy and I'm broken inside.

Bm	G

Once again I thank You

D/F#	A	G A D

Once again I pour out my life.

D	A/D G		D/F#

Now You are exalted to the highest place,

Em	D/F#	G	A

King of the heavens, where one day I'll bow.

D	A/D G		D/F#

But for now I marvel at this saving grace,

Em	Asus	D

And I'm full of praise once again,

Em	Asus	D

I'm full of praise once again.

CHORDS USED IN THIS SONG

D   A   G   Em   Asus   Bm   A/D

Matt Redman
Copyright © 1996 Kingsway's Thankyou Music
P.O. Box 75, Eastbourne, East Sussex, BN23 6NW, UK
Used by permission.

IN MY LIFE, LORD

D A Bm D/F♯
In my life, Lord,

G   Em7 C   Asus4 A
Be glorified, be glorified,

D A Bm D/F♯
In my life, Lord,

G   Asus4 A D
Be glorified   today.

CHORDS USED IN THIS SONG

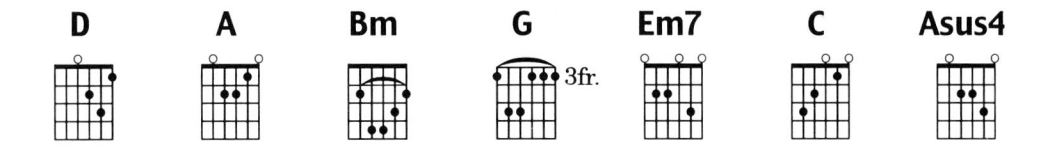

D   A   Bm   G   Em7   C   Asus4

Bob Kilpatrick
Copyright © 1978 Bob Kilpatrick Music. Administered by CopyCare
P.O. Box 77, Hailsham, East Sussex, BN27 3EF, UK
Used by permission.

RAIN AND SNOW FALL FROM THE SKY

E   C#m
Rain and snow fall from the sky, pouring down upon the earth
A   B
Causing it to spring to life, making new things come to birth.
E   C#m
And so is Your word, our Lord, it does not return to You
A   B
Having not achieved Your will; doing all You want it to.
F#m   Bsus4
We will call on You while You are near.
F#m   Bsus4
We will seek You while You may be found.

    E   A
(So) Rain down, (rain down,) rain down, (rain down,)
    C#m
Pour the water of Your Spirit
   B
On this dry and thirsty ground.
    E   A
Rain down, (rain down,) rain down, (rain down,)
    C#m
Speak Your word into our deafness.
    B
Bring Your healing to our land.
   A E
Rain down.

CHORDS USED IN THIS SONG

E C#m A B F#m Bsus4

Jamie Haith
Copyright © 1997 IQ Music Limited
Orchard House, Broad Street, Tylers Green, Cuckfield, West Sussex, RH17 5DZ, UK
Used by permission.

HERE WE STAND

Here we stand in total surrender,
Lifting our voices, abandoned to Your cause;
Here we stand, praying in the glory
Of the One and only
Jesus Christ the Lord.

> This time revival! Lord come and heal our land,
> Bring to completion
> The work that You've begun.
> This time revival! Stir up Your church again,
> Pour out Your Spirit
> On Your daughters and Your sons.

Here we stand in need of Your mercy,
Father forgive us for the time that we have lost.
Once again make us an army
To conquer this nation
With the message of the cross.

A. Piercy & C. Groves
Copyright © 1995 IQ Music Limited
Orchard House, Broad Street, Tylers Green, Cuckfield, West Sussex, RH17 5DZ, UK
Used by permission.

LORD, YOU ARE CALLING

Lord, You are calling the people of Your Kingdom
To battle in Your name against the enemy.
To stand before You a people who will serve You,
'Til Your Kingdom is released
Throughout the earth

> Let Your Kingdom come let Your will be done
> On earth as it is in heaven.
> Let Your Kingdom come let Your will be done
> On earth as it is in heaven.

At the name of Jesus every knee must bow;
The darkness of this age must flee away.
Release Your power to flow throughout the land,
Let Your glory be revealed
As we praise.

Simon & Lorraine Fenner
Copyright © 1989 Kingsway's Thankyou Music
P.O. Box 75, Eastbourne, East Sussex, BN23 6NW, UK
Used by permission.

BREATHE ON ME, BREATH OF GOD

Breathe on me, breath of God,
Fill me with life anew,
That I may love what Thou dost love
And do what Thou wouldst do.

Breathe on me, breath of God,
Until my heart is pure:
Until my will is one with Thine,
To do and to endure.

Breathe on me, breath of God,
Till I am wholly Thine,
Until this earthly part of me
Glows with Thy fire divine.

Breathe on me, breath of God,
So shall I never die,
But live with Thee the perfect life
Of Thine eternity.

E. Hatch (1878)
Public Domain

BY HIS GRACE

By His grace I am redeemed,
By His blood I am made clean,
And I now can know Him face to face.
By His power I have been raised,
Hidden now in Christ by faith.
I will praise the glory of His grace.

Steve Fry
Copyright © 1994 Deep Fryed Music. Administered by CopyCare
P.O. Box 77, Hailsham, East Sussex, BN23 3EF, UK
Used by permission.

FAITHFUL ONE

Faithful One, so unchanging,
Ageless One, You're my rock of peace.
Lord of all, I depend on You,
I call out to You again and again,
I call out to You again and again.

You are my rock in times of trouble,
You lift me up when I fall down.
All through the storm Your love is the anchor,
My hope is in You alone.

Brian Doerksen
Copyright © 1987 Mercy Publishing/Kingsway's Thankyou Music
P.O. Box 75, Eastbourne, East Sussex, BN23 6NW, UK
Used by permission.

I WILL WORSHIP

I will worship (echo)
With all of my heart. (echo)
I will praise You (echo)
With all of my strength. (all my strength)
I will seek You (echo)
All of my days. (echo)
I will follow (echo)
All of Your ways. (all Your ways)

> I will give You all my worship
> I will give You all my praise
> You alone I long to worship
> You alone are worthy of my praise

I will bow down, (echo)
Hail You as king. (echo)
I will serve You, (echo)
Give You everything. (give You everything)
I will lift up (echo)
My eyes to Your throne. (echo)
I will trust You, (echo)
I will trust You alone. (You alone)

Davis Ruis
Copyright © 1993 Shade Tree Music/Maranatha! Music. Administered by Kingsway's Thankyou Music
P.O. Box 75, Eastbourne, East Sussex, BN23 6NW, UK
Used by permission.

OVERWHELMED BY LOVE

Overwhelmed by love,
Deeper than oceans, high as the heavens.
Ever living God,
Your love has rescued me.

All my sin was laid
On Your dear Son, Your precious One.
All my debt He paid,
Great is Your love for me.

> No one could ever earn Your love,
> Your grace and mercy is free.
> Lord, these words are true,
> So is my love for You,
> So is my love for You.

Noel Richards
Copyright © 1994 Kingsway's Thankyou Music
P.O. Box 75, Eastbourne, East Sussex, BN23 6NW, UK
Used by permission.

FATHER GOD, FILL THIS PLACE

Father God, fill this place
With Your love, with Your grace.
As we call on Your name,
Visit us in power again.

Spirit come with Your peace,
Heal our wounds, bring release.
Lord, we long for Your touch,
Fill our hearts with Your love.

> Lord, we worship You.
> Lord, we worship You.

Dave Bilbrough
Copyright © 1995 Kingsway's Thankyou Music
P.O. Box 75, Eastbourne, East Sussex, BN23 6NW, UK
Used by permission.

LET ALL THE WORLD

Let all the world in every corner sing:

My God and King!

The heavens are not too high,

His praise may thither fly.

The earth is not too low,

His praises there may grow.

Let all the world in every corner sing:

My God and King!

Let all the world in every corner sing:

My God and King!

The church with psalms must shout

No door can keep them out.

But above all the heart

Must bear the longest part.

Let all the world in every corner sing:

My God and King!

George Herbert
Public Domain

WE WORSHIP AND ADORE YOU

We worship and adore You,
Lord, hear us when we call,
For there is no God above You,
You are the Lord of all.

But how can we begin to
Express what's on our hearts?
There are not words enough, Lord,
For us to even start.

The tongues of men and angels
We need, to sing your praise,
So that we may glorify Your name
Through heaven's eternal days.

There was no other good enough
To pay the price of sin;
You only could unlock the gate
Of heaven and let us in.

A. Piercy
Copyright © 1995 IQ Music Limited
Orchard House, Broad Street, Tylers Green, Cuckfield, West Sussex, RH17 5DZ, UK
Used by permission.

THE LORD IS MY LIGHT

The Lord is my light and my salvation,
Whom shall I fear?
The Lord is my strength, the strength of my life,
Whom shall I dread?

> One thing I have asked of the Lord,
> That I shall seek,
> That I may dwell in Your house all my days,
> That I may gaze on your beauty Oh Lord.

I would have despaired unless I believed
That I would see your goodness;
So I will wait, and I will be strong,
Yes I will wait for You.

Jamie Haith
Copyright © 1997 IQ Music Limited
Orchard House, Broad Street, Tylers Green, Cuckfield, West Sussex, RH17 5DZ, UK
Used by permission.

MY JESUS, MY SAVIOUR

My Jesus, my Saviour,
Lord, there is none like you.
All of my days I want to praise
The wonders of Your mighty love.
My comfort, my shelter,
Tower of refuge and strength.
Let every breath, all that I am,
Never cease to worship You.

Shout to the Lord, all the earth, let us sing:
Power and majesty, praise to the King,
Mountains bow down and the seas will roar
At the sound of Your name.
I sing for joy at the work of Your hands.
For ever I'll love You, for ever I'll stand,
Nothing compares to the promise I have in You.

Darlene Zschech
Copyright © 1993 Darlene Zschech/Hillsongs Australia. Administered by Kingsway's Thankyou Music
P.O. Box 75, Eastbourne, East Sussex, BN23 6NW, UK
Used by permission.

OUR FATHER

Our Father who art in heaven
Hallowed be Thy name.
Thy kingdom come, Thy will be done
On earth as in heaven.

Give us this day our daily bread,
And forgive our sins,
As we forgive those who sin against us.
Lead us not into temptation,
But deliver us from evil.

For Thine is the kingdom,
And the power and the glory
For ever and ever amen;
For ever and ever amen.

Simon Dixon
Copyright © 1997 IQ Music Limited
Orchard House, Broad Street, Tylers Green, Cuckfield, West Sussex, RH17 5DZ, UK
Used by permission.

I WILL OFFER UP MY LIFE

I will offer up my life in spirit and truth,
Pouring out the oil of love as my worship to You.
In surrender I must give my every part;
Lord, receive the sacrifice of a broken heart.

> Jesus what can I give, what can I bring
> To so faithful a friend, to so loving a King?
> Saviour, what can be said, what can be sung
> As a praise of Your name
> For the things You have done?
> O, my words could not tell, not even in part,
> Of the debt of love that is owed
> By this thankful heart

You deserve my every breath
For You've paid the great cost
Giving up Your life to death,
Even death on a cross.
You took all my shame away,
There defeated my sin,
Opened up the gates of heaven,
And have beckoned me in.

Matt Redman
Copyright © 1994 Kingsway's Thankyou Music
P.O. Box 75, Eastbourne, East Sussex, BN23 6NW, UK
Used by permission.

JESUS CHRIST

Jesus Christ, I think upon Your sacrifice;
You became nothing, poured out to death.
Many times I've wondered at Your gift of life,
And I'm in that place once again,
I'm in that place once again.

> And once again I look upon
> The cross where You died.
> I'm humbled by Your mercy
> And I'm broken inside.
> Once again I thank You
> Once again I pour out my life.

Now You are exalted to the highest place,
King of the heavens, where one day I'll bow.
But for now I marvel at this saving grace,
And I'm full of praise once again,
I'm full of praise once again.

Matt Redman
Copyright © 1996 Kingsway's Thankyou Music
P.O. Box 75, Eastbourne, East Sussex, BN23 6NW, UK
Used by permission.

IN MY LIFE, LORD

In my life, Lord,
Be glorified, be glorified,
In my life, Lord,
Be glorified today.

Bob Kilpatrick
Copyright © 1978 Bob Kilpatrick Music. Administered by CopyCare
P.O. Box 77, Hailsham, East Sussex, BN27 3EF, UK
Used by permission.

RAIN AND SNOW FALL FROM THE SKY

Rain and snow fall from the sky,
Pouring down upon the earth
Causing it to spring to life,
Making new things come to birth.
And so is Your word, our Lord,
It does not return to You
Having not achieved Your will;
Doing all You want it to.

We will call on You while You are near.
We will seek You while You may be found.

> Rain down, (rain down,)
> Rain down, (rain down,)
> Pour the water of Your Spirit
> On this dry and thirsty ground.
> Rain down, (rain down,)
> Rain down, (rain down,)
> Speak Your word into our deafness.
> Bring Your healing to our land.
> Rain down.

Jamie Haith
Copyright © 1997 IQ Music Limited
Orchard House, Broad Street, Tylers Green, Cuckfield, West Sussex, RH17 5DZ, UK
Used by permission.